THANK You for your concern,
PRAYERS, + love over my
troubled YEARS. You HAVE been
A Blessing to me

LOVE TANTA

Christmas 2003

© 2002 by Barbour Publishing, Inc.

ISBN 1-58660-901-7

Scripture quotations marked NLT are taken from the *Holy Bible,* New Living Translation, copyright © 1996. Used by permission of Tyndale House Publishers, Inc. Wheaton, Illinois 60189, U.S.A. All rights reserved.

Scripture quotations marked NIV are taken from the HOLY BIBLE, NEW INTERNATIONAL VERSION®. NIV®. Copyright © 1973, 1978, 1984 by International Bible Society. Used by permission of Zondervan Publishing House. All rights reserved.

Scripture quotations marked NRSV are taken from the New Revised Standard Version Bible, copyright © 1989, Division of Christian Education of the National Council of the Churches of Christ in the United States of America. Used by permission. All rights reserved.

Selections on pages 15, 24–25, 32, and 35 are by Viola Ruelke Gommer and are used with the author's permission.

Published by Humble Creek, P.O. Box 719, Uhrichsville, Ohio 44683.

Printed in China.
5 4 3 2 1

With Sincere Gratitude

ELLYN SANNA

HUMBLECREEK
INSPIRATION FOR LIFE

*Gratitude is
the heart's memory.*

FRENCH PROVERB

*I*thank my God every time I remember you.
PHILIPPIANS 1:3 NRSV

I am grateful for. . .

- the joy you have shared with me;

- the hope you have given me;

- the kindness you have shown me; and

- the generous spirit you never fail to offer.

Gratitude is born in hearts
that take time to
count up past mercies.

CHARLES E. JEFFERSON

1

The Joy You Share

When we're together,
everything seems more fun.
Jokes make me laugh more,
the sun shines brighter,
and even ice cream tastes sweeter than before.
When I'm feeling gloomy,
you shine your joy into my heart.
Thank you.

I have found that
there is a tremendous joy
in giving.

WILLIAM BLACK

*J*oy is the echo of
God's life within us.
JOSEPH MARMION

With Sincere Gratitude—9

*J*oy is prayer.
Joy is strength.
Joy is love.
Joy is a net of love by which you can catch souls.
She gives most who gives with joy.

MOTHER TERESA

*A joyful and pleasant thing
it is to be thankful.*

PRAYER BOOK

*T*he longer I know you,
the more I learn. . .
about you
and myself
and life
and God.
Knowing you has taught me so much.
You fill my life with delight,
and I am filled with gratitude.

. . .like going on a treasure hunt.
What wonderful
worlds we can find
in others!

EDWARD E. FORD

With Sincere Gratitude—11

*T*he words *thank* and *think*
come from the same Latin word.
No wonder then
whenever I think of you
I give thanks.
You give me joy.

*I would maintain that thanks
are the highest form of thought,
and that gratitude is
happiness doubled
by wonder.*

G. K. CHESTERTON

2

The Hope You Give

*Your love has given me
great joy and encouragement.*

PHILEMON 7 NIV

*T*hank you for seeing potential in me.
With your encouragement,
I see opportunities ahead
and hope in my future.

When darkness isolated me from everyone,
you were the gift that brought light to my life.
When silence surrounded me,
your words of encouragement and understanding
reached into my heart.
You turned shadows into sunlight
and silence into song.
Now I am no longer alone.
Thank you
from my heart
to yours.

Sometimes our light goes out
but is blown into flame
by another human being.
Each of us owes the deepest thanks to
those who have rekindled this light.

ALBERT SCHWEITZER

I am grateful
for all the times
you rekindled my flickering flame.
Thank you for blowing
the breath of hope into my life.

*H*ope is like the sun, which,
as we journey toward it,
casts the shadow of our burden behind us.
SAMUEL SMILES

*There is no place
more delightful than hope.*

CICERO

*H*ope quickens all
the still parts of life
and keeps the mind awake. . . .
JOSEPH ADDISON

To pray together. . .
is the most tender
brotherhood of hope.

MADAME DE STAEL

*W*hen I was ready to give up hope,
thank you for praying for me
and with me. . .
encouraging me
to hope again.

Hope springs exulting on triumphant wings.

ROBERT BURNS

Hope ever urges on. . . .

ALBIUS TIBULLUS

Hope awakens courage. . . .

KARL VON KNEBEL

*H*ope is the belief,
more or less strong, that joy will come.

SYDNEY SMITH

Hope does not disappoint us.

ROMANS 5:5 NIV

Eternity is the divine treasure house,
and hope is the window,
by means of which
mortals are permitted to see,
as through a glass darkly,
the things which God is preparing.

WILLIAM MOUNTFORD

*S*haring happiness with others
may seem like such a little thing.
But it's not. The joy you give
not only brightens my day;
it also builds my faith
and helps me see
God's kingdom,
real, alive, and shining,
in the midst of my ordinary life.

3

The Kindness You Show

Your door swings wide,
your arms open,
and a chair waits just for me.
A pot of tea is ready,
and all these say
"Welcome,"
"Come, rest,"
"Find peace."

$\mathcal{A}$s we sip our tea, you listen to more than my words.
You hear my heart,
and your words in return speak
comfort, understanding, and wisdom.
All these say "Welcome."
All these say "Love."
Through you I see God.
Through you I find rest and serenity.
Through you I know God's love.
My spirit is renewed.

With Sincere Gratitude—25

*S*ome days God seems so far away
I wonder if His love is real.
And then your kindness touches my life.
God reaches out to me through you,
and then I understand how much
the Creator of the universe
cares for me.
Thank you
for being
God's hands.
Thank you
for demonstrating His love.

One looks back with. . .
gratitude to those who
touched our human feelings.

CARL JUNG

The heart benevolent and kind
The most resembles God.
ROBERT BURNS

Kind words are the music of the world.
They have a power which seems to be
beyond natural causes,
as if they were some angel's song which
had lost its way and come on earth.

FREDERICK WILLIAM FABER

Whosoever takes up the burden of his neighbor. . .
and ministers unto those in need
out of the abundance of things he
has received. . .
of God's bounty—this man. . .
is an imitator of God.

DIOGNETUS

*T*hank you for your kindness,
for it has lightened the burden I was carrying.
Though you may have thought your action was small and
insignificant,
you have made my life easier.
Thank you for caring enough about me
to give yourself.

*Charity is above all
a hymn of love.
Real, pure love is
the gift of oneself.*

PIUS XII

*I*n all things we learn only from those we love.
GOETHE

Hand grasps hand, eye lights eye. . .
And great hearts expand,
And grow. . .

ROBERT BROWNING

*Y*our kindness has taught me far
more
than any teacher.
Thank you for your many lessons of
love.

4

The Generosity You Offer

*G*enerous hearts
share whatever they have,
affirm and validate the good in others,
give freely,
provide wise counsel,
have open hands,
and are generous to all they meet.
You have a generous heart,
and I am grateful.

*No one has ever become
poor by giving.*

ANNE FRANK

*G*od has given us two hands—
one to receive with and the other to give with.
We are not cisterns
made for hoarding;
we are channels made for sharing.
BILLY GRAHAM

*H*appy are those who fear the LORD. . . .
When darkness overtakes [them],
light will come bursting in.
They are generous, compassionate, and righteous.
All goes well for those who are generous,
who lend freely and conduct their business fairly. . . .
They do not fear bad news;
they confidently trust the LORD to care for them.
They are confident and fearless
and can face their foes triumphantly.
They give generously to those in need.
Their good deeds will never be forgotten.
They will have influence and honor. . . .

Praise the LORD!

PSALM 112: 1, 4–5, 7–9; 113:1 NLT

When you give,
there are no strings attached.
You give with no thought of return,
no debt incurred,
and your giving nourishes my spirit.
I am free to pass your gifts
on to another
. . .and another
. . .and another,
a chain of lives linked
and changed by
your giving spirit.

If you give, you will receive.
Your gift will return to you in full measure, pressed down,
shaken together to make room for more, and running over.
Whatever measure you use in giving—large or small—
it will be used to measure what is given back to you.

LUKE 6:38 NLT

The generous prosper and are satisfied;
those who refresh others
will themselves
be refreshed.

PROVERBS 11:25 NLT

Giving is the secret of a happy life.
Not necessarily money,
but whatever a man has
of encouragement and sympathy
and understanding.

JOHN D. ROCKEFELLER, JR.

*T*here are three kinds of giving: grudge giving, duty giving, and thanksgiving. Grudge giving says, "I hate to," duty giving says, "I ought to," thanksgiving says "I want to." The first comes from constraint, the second from a sense of obligation, the third from a full heart. Nothing much is conveyed in grudge giving, since "the gift without the giver is bare." Something more happens in duty giving but there is no song in it. Thanksgiving is an open gate into the love of God.

ROBERT N. RODENMAYER

Thank you for giving so freely to me.
Your generosity has opened
a gate in my heart
and God's love
has come in.

$\mathcal{L}$et us be grateful to people who make us happy;
they are the charming gardeners who make our souls bloom.

MARCEL PROUST

*Gratitude is the fairest blossom
which springs from the soul.*

HENRY WARD BEECHER

$\mathcal{T}$hank you for all you have done to
help me bloom.

We have not made ourselves;
we are the gift of
the living God to one another.

REINE DUELL BETHANY

I am sincerely grateful
for the gift God gave to me
through you!